WEALTH WISE, A NOVEL

First Printing, 2023

First Printing, 2023

"My Lord, enable me to be grateful for Your favor which You have bestowed upon me and upon my parents and to do righteousness of which You approve. And admit me by Your mercy into [the ranks of] Your righteous servants." - from Al-Qur'an, Surah an-Naml ayat 19

"ëlëk du añ du rer, waaye lu mëtë seed la."
(You always prepare for tomorrow,
because you never know what to expect.)
- Wolof proverb

Wealth Wise, A Novel

FINANCIAL JOURNEY
SERIES VOLUME 1

Wolof of Wall Street

Ndeye Diop

Samawat Press

Contents

Foreword

Spoiler alert: In this book, the Wolof of Wall Street provides you with simple guidelines to wealth wisdom that most schools don't!

Imagine, for a moment, standing on the golden sands of a serene beach, the waves gently lapping at your feet. A stranger approaches, holding out a rough, unassuming stone. To the untrained eye, it might seem like just another rock, but to those who know, it's a diamond in the rough. This diamond, raw and untouched, represents the potential wealth that lies within each individual and each family. Just as a diamond requires careful cutting, shaping, and polishing to reveal its true brilliance, so too does wealth education, wealth understanding, and wealth generation. You need guidance to generate wealth and this is what you will get by reading this.

The family, with its deep-rooted values, traditions, and bonds, is like the skilled artisan that shapes this diamond, ensuring that each facet reflects light, creating a dazzling display of brilliance. Building wealth is not merely about accumulating material riches; it is about understanding the game, and the principles behind each financial instrument that is at your disposal. It is about understanding the value of relationships, the importance of legacy, and the role of the family as the cornerstone of prosperity. It is also about understanding thoroughly the systems that allow you to generate wealth. Just as a diamond is formed under pressure and becomes one of the most coveted jewels in the world, as it goes through polishing phases, families, through challenges and adversities, have the potential to harness their collective strength and shine brightly in the realm of wealth creation.

They need to educate themselves on how this is achieved. To achieve this they need a plain, simple, easy-to-understand roadmap. "Wealth Wise" provides this roadmap in a way that is simple to apprehend and understand, concrete, and readily actionable.

As you delve into the pages of this book, remember the diamond metaphor. Recognize the power of learning and education for you and your family unit in building your wealth and gaining wealth wisdom. Recognize the power of the family unit to build generational wealth and in shaping your future and the future of your family. Understand that the journey to prosperity is an individual effort, that can benefit the collective if it's taught and passed through generations properly.

May this book serve as a guide, illuminating the path to wealth and prosperity, it is meant to be such a tool for you.

-Gilles Amadou Acogny & Wali Adeola Acogny

Acknowledgement

All praises are due to the Creator, The Enricher.

To my Mother, Angelique, oh how I wish you were here to witness me pursuing my purpose. I am often called resilient and driven but I, without a doubt, give all that credit to you. You encouraged my siblings and me to always put in our best effort and keep our heads high, knowing no matter the outcome we did our best. Your prayers and motivation will forever be the fuel that keeps me going. Merci Mendy Docteur.

To my Father Assane, my role model. You introduced my love of literature to me. Made me inquisitive, which led to this. I aspire to be half the person you are. Thank you.

To my WHY, Mairame and Amina, I hope the guidance and words in this book make you proud to be my children. I pray that you utilize it for your benefit and become the savvy and sophisticated young woman I know you are.

To my older sisters, Oumou and Dieynaba, my bonus mothers. I can loudly say that all the good things I am aside from my Lord are by your influence. For that I thank you.

My friends, my chosen family, the people who believe in me more than I do myself at times, I wouldn't trade you for the world. Kuu lim joom (whoever lists omits).

Lastly, to the person holding this book, may you find beneficial wisdom that will help you, your family, and your community.

1

The Wolof of Wall Street

Imaan exhaled as she strolled down Linden Lane one last time, diploma in hand and dreams in her heart. Freshly graduated from Boston College with a degree in Political Science, she was standing on the precipice of a new journey. Within her was a deep-seated aspiration to attain financial freedom by age 40. She knew that the path would not be easy, but she approached it with unwavering determination, full of hope. Inspired by the wisdom of her mother, Angelique, and the support of her mentors, this was one journey she was more than willing to take.

Angelique, the matriarch of this narrative, had emigrated to the United States from Senegal, a West African nation about the size of South Dakota. In Senegal, financial literacy was not openly discussed, an unspoken taboo in her community. As a child, Angelique received no formal or informal education in personal finance. Witnessing the standard reliance on adult children as a retirement plan left a lasting mark on her. Without positive wealth preservation examples to follow from home, her first years in America were marred by financial missteps – overspending, insufficient savings, and a fear of investing.

Angelique's transformation began when she broke free from the cycle of living from one paycheck to the next, a cycle driven by her tendencies for extravagance. With a stable income, she diligently paid off her student loans and department store credit cards. Yet, her mission extended beyond personal redemption. She was determined to equip her children with financial knowledge and good habits so they wouldn't face the same struggles she had. She embarked on a pursuit of financial knowledge, devouring books and articles, and even making a career pivot into the world of Wall Street.

Over time, Angelique became a beacon of financial literacy, guiding her family and friends on the journey to fiscal responsibility. She shared her knowledge about budgeting, saving, investing, and safeguarding finances from fraud, empowering those around her with the tools to make informed financial decisions based on what they truly value.

In the stories of Imaan and Angelique, we see the enduring power of education, determination, and the legacy of wisdom passed from one generation to another. It is a testament to the potential for transformation, and the importance of equipping our children with the knowledge and habits they need to thrive in a complex financial world.

I wrote this book because I want to help other people from underprivileged backgrounds learn financial literacy so that they can make better financial decisions and build wealth for themselves and their families. We are only as strong as the communities we build.

Money matters can be intimidating but with proper education it can be mastered. If you have felt like you had no clue where to even start or are just eager to expand your knowledge about finances, then this book is for you.

2

Wealth Wise

As Imaan rode the train back home to Virginia from Boston, she thought about how to start her financial journey. At that moment, she took out her journal and started writing what she would later dub her "Wealth Wise Manifesto".

"Wealth can be defined in different ways, depending on the context. A proper personal understanding is important before embarking on a journey to financial freedom. Some people define wealth as net worth. I will look at wealth as the amount of time my needs can be met without working. A way to build wealth is by owning assets that earn income while I sleep. It is important to remember, that money or status by themselves do not equal wealth. Money is a means of exchanging time for wealth. If I have a high income with high expenses, I will probably not be wealthy. Status is a station in the social hierarchy. 10 million followers online may sound alluring, but if it cannot be monetized, that is not wealth. So, it's possible to have lots of both and little wealth. But both can be used to attain wealth if proper knowledge is applied. Wealth can be generated ethically, and I do not like the idea of material gains being attained immorally. Finally, if I harbor jealousy for people who have what I do not, or question whether they deserve it, wealth will elude me.

Life becomes fulfilling when we understand the concept of compound returns. Being wealth-wise means understanding that we want passive growth of our financial assets so that we can focus more time on other aspects of life we value. You're not going to become wealthy by only renting out your time for a wage or salary. Earned income must be used to own pieces of growing businesses and to purchase income-producing assets. When you invest your money wisely and earn consistent returns over time, those returns can compound, meaning they generate more returns. This effect can significantly increase your wealth over the long term. But remember that you may also have to overcome some personal issues with overspending, debt, or lack of focus.

Also, expressing gratitude for what I have is crucial before expecting more of it. Whatever good I have, recognize it as such. Yes, hard work matters, but whether one believes in a Merciful and Gracious Creator or not, showing gratitude for what we currently have allows us to recognize the good in our lives and create the mindset to be able to receive more with grace.

Another way to enrich our lives is to realize compound returns through our life experiences. This happens when we invest time and effort in building trust and meaningful relationships with family and friends. The more trust you establish in your key relationships, the stronger and more fulfilling they become, creating a solid foundation in your inner circle. Engaging in meaningful and positive experiences together, such as travel, hobbies, or pursuing common goals, can strengthen the bond with family and friends. These shared experiences create lasting memories and support the connection, deepening the relationship over time.

Compound returns also come from dedicating time and effort to learning and skill development. Consistent accumulation of knowledge builds upon itself, and when applied to my life, knowledge becomes wisdom. Each new piece of information or skill acquired builds upon the previous ones, allowing you to grasp complex concepts more easily and become more proficient in a particular field.

Combining knowledge from multiple disciplines can also lead to accelerated growth. By integrating different areas of expertise, you can gain unique insights, and problem-solving abilities, and innovate in ways that are not possible by focusing on a single domain. For example, you cook for a food truck you own and can also effectively promote your brand, marketing the menu around town. You developed mastery in two areas that will help your business grow faster. Mastery of different skill sets also allows you to retain more profit than if you had to pay a brand manager or marketing employee. This is not to say that as a business owner, you must do everything yourself. We need to recognize when tasks should be outsourced to professionals or remain "in-house" to gain efficiencies or capital. But if you have a passion or interest in something, why not take some time to learn about it and see where it goes?

Initiating generational wealth requires an individual or family to acquire knowledge and apply it by walking through specific steps in the wealth-building process. This is how to become wealth-wise. Generational wealth requires imparting that wisdom to the next generation so that wealth preservation and growth continue, therefore controlling the urge to only consume and pleasure seek. This wisdom will help you, your family, and your community for generations. The new generation applies that wisdom by walking through many of the same necessary steps of growth and preservation. This wisdom is rooted in investing in knowledge, family, values, and health. If done correctly, it should not be as hard to maintain the wealth as it was to initially build its foundations."

We will follow Imaan, our bright young woman fresh out of college, on her financial journey. She is eager to trek into the world of finance and investing. Armed with wisdom passed down from her mother, she is fueled by a strong desire to build a secure future and has carefully devised a plan.

3

Risk Management

Imaan embarked on her professional career as a political analyst, fully aware of the challenges and opportunities that lay ahead. Additionally, she understood the importance of financial literacy and sought advice from her mother and other trusted mentors, individuals whose wisdom had guided her throughout her life.

Imaan was keen on managing her investments wisely, ensuring that her hard-earned capital was put to work in a way that would secure her financial future. Her mentors played a pivotal role in helping her navigate the complex landscape of financial risk. They shared their insights on the art of diversifying portfolios and spreading investments across different assets to mitigate risk and maximize potential returns. They patiently explained the intricacies of the market, simplifying its complexities and empowering her with knowledge. Their guidance became her compass as she ventured into the uncertain waters of financial risk. Imaan's commitment to learning and her mother's advice would serve as the foundation upon which she built her financial security, ensuring that her journey would be marked by informed decisions and a clear path to her financial goals.

She learned that an often-overlooked aspect of financial freedom is risk management. Being wealth-wise is driven by a mindset that emphasizes being strategic, disciplined, and managing risk. It means understanding that no one is more responsible, accountable, and capable of protecting your financial health than you. Although we may not call it that, we manage risk in our lives daily. Keeping our passwords private, locking our doors, and keeping the location feature turned on in our children's mobile devices are all forms of protecting what you value, also known as risk management. Managing financial risk involves taking steps to minimize the negative impact of uncertain events on your finances. We minimize our risky financial activities by having a vision, controlling spending, developing passive income, and saving. Financial risk management is an ongoing process that requires periodic evaluation and adjustment as circumstances change. Financial freedom is based on the ability to take calculated risks and have discipline.

Budgeting, a financial risk management essential, will help you track income and expenses, ensuring that money is allocated wisely and essentials are prioritized. Imaan decided to start an emergency fund called a financial shield, that will provide a safety net for unexpected expenses or income disruptions, such as medical bills or job loss. Debt management will help maintain a manageable level of debt and make timely payments to reduce financial risks associated with high-interest rates and potential default on loans. Investment planning, including setting financial goals and developing a long-term plan will help determine how much savings she will need in retirement, when she can retire, and other wealth-building strategies.

FBI of Financial Freedom

Drawing from a successful tactic she had used in her many classes, Imaan decided to create an acronym to help her remember the important risk management principles she learned about. She adopted the well-known acronym, FBI, to develop a framework through which she could safeguard her financial well-being through budgeting and analysis, minimizing debt, and informed investing. Flexibility. Balance.

Integrity. Like the Federal Bureau of Investigation (FBI), she would conduct thorough investigations (into her financial decisions), making informed choices to achieve long-lasting financial freedom. By being open to alternative approaches, diversifying income streams, and embracing innovative solutions, she knew she could maintain a resilient and adaptable financial base.

F is for Flexibility – This principle recognizes the importance of maintaining a flexible financial approach that allows for adaptation as Imaan matures, her family grows, and priorities change. This is accomplished by adjusting financial strategies to changing circumstances while still being true to your overall vision. Flexibility allows her to respond effectively to unexpected events, such as job loss or market fluctuations, without jeopardizing financial security.

B is for Balance – This principle addresses the need to weigh immediate financial necessities (short term) against future aspirations (long term). It helps Imaan answer questions like, "How do I pay my bills now and also save for a house?" Sticking to a balanced budget allows her income to flow where it is needed, prioritizing essential expenses, saving, and funding her vision as a whole to realize long-term dreams.

I is for Integrity – This principle is the FBI mindset at its core. It emphasizes ethical and honest behavior when it comes to money matters. This involves making honest financial decisions based on her values. Integrity in finance means avoiding fraudulent schemes, dishonest practices, or taking advantage of others for personal gain. This mentality helps protect Imaan from being victimized by "furus" (financial gurus) and online influencers with self-proclaimed secret knowledge about how to achieve zero risk, 1,000 percent returns on investments. Maintaining integrity in finances shields her vision from being sidetracked by greed, excess spending, and emergencies. She feels like financial integrity at the individual level will also contribute to a more reliable financial environment that benefits society.

4

Financial Shield Account

Understanding the importance of an emergency fund is a fundamental step toward financial security. Imaan immediately recognized this after the first time her car broke down and she needed to pay for the repairs with money she was saving for a trip to Ghana with friends. She realized that life is unpredictable, and unforeseen circumstances can arise at any moment. So, with renewed discipline and unwavering determination, she set out to build a safety net that would shield her from the storms of life. Imaan's dedication led her to diligently save, setting aside enough resources to provide a cushion for whatever challenges lay ahead. She understood that this financial resilience was not just about protecting herself but also ensuring stability for her future. It was a testament to her foresight and commitment to securing her own well-being and peace of mind, no matter what life might throw her way.

Imaan imagined other big, unplanned expenses that could arise like a home repair, or worse yet, the loss of a job. The thought of not being prepared again scared her, and she wanted to confidently handle this type of event in the future. She considered her options. She could put big charges on a credit card or pull from savings that she was growing specifically to make a down payment on her first home. Imaan decided that instead of raiding her savings every time a calamity hit, she could establish some financial security in advance. Financial freedom begins with being able to deploy a financial defense system that protects us head-on against emergencies that can disrupt our lives. Some may like considering it an emergency fund, but she called it a financial shield. It's a rainy-day fund, but much more, because some events can cause storms that have us struggling to keep our head above water for weeks or months depending on how prepared we are. Here's how Imaan started her financial shield account:

1. Set up a separate, liquid emergency-only savings account.
2. Contributed to that account regularly. This was done by paying herself first by scheduling a biweekly or monthly automatic transfer.
3. Started by saving $1,000.
4. The next goal was to work toward saving three months of living expenses, then six months, and finally twenty-four months. How much was three months of her living expenses? She calculated that from knowing what is in her needs bucket when she built her budget. Later we will discuss the ins and outs of her budgeting but in general, living expenses include:
   - housing
   - food
   - transportation
   - medical
   - utilities including phone/internet
   - essential debt

Don't think you can even save $1,000? Imaan encouraged her friends to use this twelve-month savings challenge as a motivating and effective way to kick off their financial shield accounts:

**12 MONTH FINANCIAL SHIELD
SAVINGS EXERCISE**

Another invaluable concept that Imaan inherited from her mother was the tradition known as "natt" in Wolof, a form of crowdfunding deeply rooted in Senegalese culture.

Here's how it works: A group of individuals come together, each committing to contribute a fixed amount of money monthly. Every month, the entire collected sum goes to one of the participants. So, let's say 10 people decide to pool $500 each for 10 months. Every month, one of them would receive the full $5,000 until each participant was funded.

This is an interest-free loan system and serves as an ingenious alternative to traditional saving and borrowing. Remarkably, this practice has endured for centuries among Senegalese women, embodying the strength of communal support and financial solidarity.

Imaan wisely harnessed the power of "natt" to accelerate the funding of her financial shield account. She also used this method to fund other endeavors and even coordinated one to gather the down payment for a new family home. It's a testament to the enduring wisdom of shared financial responsibility and the innovative ways in which communities come together to secure their futures.

5

'Til Debt Do Us Part

One of Imaan's mentors once told her to remember that debt has its purpose. It can help you access opportunities that benefit your future if used strategically. When debt is used to buy assets that will make more money, it is called leverage. Oftentimes debt is needed to acquire a personal vehicle or mortgage for our primary residence. Although cars and homes may be a necessity, they may actually become more of a burden depending on how they are used. A car with a high monthly payment, high insurance costs, and rapidly depreciating in value is not an asset of the income-generating kind, especially if it is for personal use, like commuting to work. If you have a primary residence with a mortgage, property taxes, and maintenance costs, it should be considered an illiquid asset at best, if it's not generating rental income.

Another important thing she learned about debt is that it is her responsibility to keep her use of it under control, no matter how alluring it may be. A significant factor in most modern-day financial crises has been unsustainable debt levels and excessive borrowing by households, businesses, and governments. Debt is a risk that must be managed because when you borrow to buy something, you do not own it outright until that loan is paid off. If you don't make your loan payments, your lender eventually has the right to take it.

Consumer lending is a multi-trillion-dollar industry that encompasses various loans such as mortgages, personal loans, credit cards, and student loans. The targeted customer base of the financial services industry is essentially everyone with a heartbeat. How so? Who won't eventually need a home, car, or student loan in their life? Banks have developed products, sales, marketing, and other psychological persuasion tactics to convince consumers that they can afford more debt, thus maximizing their own net interest income. Net interest income is the excess revenue generated from the interest that banks earn on loans minus the interest they pay on customer deposits. It can often represent half of a bank's overall revenue. They charge higher interest rates for loans than the interest rates they offer consumers on deposits because they strive to maximize profit on this type of revenue in a pool of ever-growing would-be debtors.

In early 2023, the national average 30-year fixed mortgage APR was seven percent. For a home purchased on these terms for $300,000, with a twenty percent down payment, the buyer would end up paying over $334,000 in interest payments alone by the conclusion of the term.

Then there is bad debt like store-issued credit cards. Watching her friends' spending habits, Imaan realized that financing should be reserved for purchasing a home or business opportunity, not a meal at your favorite restaurant. Interest steals your income. Imagine the havoc a 19% APR (the average interest rate on credit cards in the fourth quarter of 2022) on credit cards can wreak on your finances. Thirty-five percent of Americans carry a month-to-month balance which accrues interest. In 2020, American banks made $76 billion in revenue from interest fees off consumers.

If not careful, leveraging debt can encourage you to spend more than you can afford. When a person is given a chance to make purchases on debt, they tend to lose track of their financial capabilities and spend beyond their means. Banks want you to borrow money because they make more revenue as borrowing increases.

Your credit score can suffer as well, so you should never borrow all the way up to the limit you have been approved at.

Imaan looked at debt through the FBI framework and strove to eliminate current personal debt and examine the need for future debt. Excessive debt can destabilize your financial flexibility, balance, and integrity. When you have high levels of debt, your financial strategy becomes inflexible and stagnates. A significant portion of your income is dedicated to merely paying the minimum monthly balance due. An ill-timed unexpected event on top of high debt payments can destabilize what little financial stability you thought you had. High debt levels also make it difficult to maintain balance. When you're burdened with debt but have no strategy to get rid of it, your attention is diverted to the short-term, leaving long-term goals unattended. And when debt becomes an overwhelming expense in your budget, you may be tempted to resort to perceived shortcuts such as get-rich-quick schemes or gambling in the stock market to supplement your income, further degrading your financial integrity.

Unhealthy debt keeps you from realizing your vision. When we define a vision, we are imagining where we will be at a given point in the future. But when we are in too much debt, we don't get to achieve that goal at the time we want or sometimes at all. This can lead to depression and anxiety. Finally, Imaan remembered some of the stories her mother shared with her on some of the physical health issues like migraines and high blood pressure that can come because of stressing over debt.

6

Budgeting

Budgeting became Imaan's secret weapon in her pursuit of financial freedom. She approached her finances with meticulous care, recognizing that every dollar held the potential to shape her future.

She diligently tracked her expenses, scrutinized every line item, and made tough decisions to cut out unnecessary costs.

In her world, every dollar had a purpose, a role to play in her journey toward long-term financial security. She often remembers her mother's favorite line of questioning when she wanted to buy something she wanted. "How much of your precious time will you have to trade to buy this? Instead of looking at items in dollars, look at the time it takes you to earn that amount of money and determine if the time sacrificed would be worth obtaining it."

For instance, Imaan wants to buy a pair of new shoes that cost $200. She currently works a job paying $30/hour. In reality, it will cost her over 6 hours of her working day for that one pair of shoes. Analyzing her wants allowed her to reconsider spending money on items she ultimately deemed not worth her time.

She understood that discipline and foresight were essential tools in achieving her goals. A world-class athlete once said, "Discipline is doing what you hate to do but doing it like you love it." That's the level of dedication required to be the best. So, she kept her eyes steadfastly fixed on that long-term prize, unwavering in her commitment to financial responsibility and the brighter future it promised.

Imaan's story is a testament to the power of prudent financial management, a reminder that with dedication and a well-structured plan, anyone can chart a course toward the financial freedom they desire.

Budgeting is the disciplined process and plan to clearly define how you will use your income. It doesn't have to be perfect, but Imaan did her best to adhere to it as much as she could. After establishing and analyzing a budget, she started to see where her income goes every month. Without a budget, it was almost impossible to know this. A budget helped her understand if where she spent her money was helping her live according to her vision. It helped her set simple financial freedom goals and organize them because her resources and vision were unified.

Let's pause here. Do you have a vision? When there is no vision, we don't understand our higher objectives for that which we value like family, health, spirituality, security, pursuing purpose, and community. The result is that most of your spending ends up being a reaction to impulses or emergencies (yours or those of others).

When Imaan first developed her budget, she wrote down her values and then wrote down at least three important things for each of those values. For example, she wanted to be open about money with her children and be able to vacation in places that rejuvenate. She wanted the ability to spend time in worship without feeling rushed. She wanted to invest in projects that enhanced her community long after she was gone.

Everyone has different priorities, so your budget is guided by your vision which is your intentional statement on what's important to you. It's crucial to establish a budget that works for your situation and goals.

After consulting her mother, Imaan created a budget that allowed her to comfortably contribute to her investment portfolio each month. She diligently saved a portion of her income from her entry-level job, ensuring she had enough for her living expenses while setting aside funds for investments.

Imaan's budgeting enabled her to track her expenses, keep them low, drive them lower, and determine what she could afford to spend money on. She tracked the progress she'd made toward making her vision a reality. Her vision `influenced her budget because she made intentional decisions on investing, giving, and consuming. A good budget is divided into four or five primary categories, where income is allocated in percentages.

- **Income** is the incoming after-tax money used to distribute money to other categories.
- **Savings** is the "pay yourself first" bucket, which you fund automatically from your income. This includes investments. Converting earned income into assets is the biggest key to building wealth. 25-30% is a target allocation.
- **Needs** are the everyday essentials and paying your bills bucket.50-55% is a target allocation.
- **Giving** is the help others bucket. 5% is a target allocation. (Optional but sharing from your sustenance is important to financial freedom)
- **Wants** are for your recreation, entertainment, and splurging. Wants are unlimited so be mindful here. Transferring savings to this category is not a good idea. 15% is a target allocation.

Imaan initially had trouble identifying investment funds for her Savings bucket. After identifying her Wants bucket based on the last three months of expenses, she diverted half of that total every single month into investing in something that produces income instead.

People usually find several small items like subscriptions and coffee to cut down on. But most people are paying too much for their car, home, or food and that is a big reason why their budgeted

Needs are over 50% of their income. A big part of understanding debt is to stop assuming that big purchases require debt. It's possible to pay cash for a decent used car. Imaan bought her first car with cash by working as a waitress in college. She was determined to graduate from college without debt after her mother told her that the interest accumulated on car loans prevented many people from fully enjoying their lives after landing their first job. It just takes time, patience, and most importantly a willingness to fight the impulse to buy a new vehicle as opposed to a cheaper, older, yet reliable model.

Imaan also read that unaddressed debt is the reason most budgeting efforts fail. One cause is that the budget can become over-inflated. When lenders issue us credit, our real income does not increase but mentally we may feel like it has. She thought of it as being a prisoner to the lender. Our needs have increased because at least the minimum monthly payment for each loan or credit card balance must be paid to the lender until that debt is paid down to zero. Paying only the minimum monthly amount due on loans allows more interest to be accrued which means it will take longer to pay off. Imaan didn't want debt stealing from her future self because being in debt means future income is already allocated to future needs. This prevents you from funding future savings, wants, and community endeavors. Future income is not promised, so this introduces risk to our lives because it's spending money you have not yet earned.

7

Debt Payoff

Imaan always uses a debt payoff template to see how much interest she is paying, create a payoff strategy, and track her progress. There are different approaches to debt settlement. The method of starting from the smaller debt to the bigger debt is called the snowball approach. This was Imaan's preferred method because that way, she felt like she was taking small wins very quickly. There's also the avalanche approach that requires you to start with the debt that has the biggest accumulated interest.

There are several debt payoff strategies you can choose from to effectively manage and eliminate your debt. Here are some commonly used approaches:

1. Snowball Method: This strategy focuses on paying off debts in order of smallest balance to largest balance, regardless of interest rates. The idea is to gain momentum and motivation by paying off smaller debts first, then rolling the payments into larger debts. As each debt is paid off, the freed-up cash flow is applied to the next debt.
2. Avalanche Method: Unlike the snowball method, the avalanche method prioritizes paying off debts with the highest interest rates first. By targeting debts with higher interest

rates, you can minimize the overall interest paid and potentially save more money in the long run. It may take longer to see the results compared to the snowball method, but it can be more cost-effective.

3. Bi-Weekly Payments: Instead of making monthly payments, some people opt for bi-weekly payments. By doing so, they end up making an extra payment each year, reducing the overall term of the loan and potentially saving on interest costs.

During periods of debt payoff, Imaan tried to cut down on spending and review her budget to find more money that could go towards eliminating debt. Aside from cutting expenses, she asked for a 10% raise every year and tried earning some extra money which would be solely for repaying debts. Offering freelance services, looking for side gigs, selling what she could sell, and just making sure she's doing something to bring more money in. Ditching debt takes commitment, hard work, and willpower. Early in her debt payoff struggles it seemed like it was taking forever and she was not making much progress. But she did not give up, remembering that eliminating debt is a major step towards realizing her vision.

A gem she took from her mother was that it is important to assess your financial situation and goals when choosing a debt payoff strategy. What works for one person may not be suitable for another. Consider factors like interest rates, total debt amount, and personal discipline, before deciding on the most appropriate strategy for your circumstances.

8

Simple Investing

Although Imaan had taken a few finance courses in college and learned the basics of investing from her mother, she decided to educate herself on various investment options. She attended seminars, read books, and sought mentors from amongst experienced investors. She learned about stocks, mutual funds, and real estate. She also sought the advice of a financial coach before finalizing her strategy. This helped her understand the importance of diversification and decided to invest in a mix of asset classes to mitigate risk.

Imaan came to understand that long-term investing is a cornerstone of financial growth. She recognized that building wealth required a patient approach, so she started methodically investing in low-cost index funds and stocks. She also explored real estate investment trusts (REITs) as a way to invest in the property market without the need for direct ownership.

Over time, Imaan's investments began to bear fruit. Her portfolio grew steadily as she reinvested dividends and capitalized on market opportunities. She maintained a realistic expectation of returns and didn't succumb to get-rich-quick schemes or impulsive trading decisions. She understood that the journey to financial security was a marathon, not a sprint.

Her knowledge and resilience became her shield against the inevitable market fluctuations that are part of investing in any market landscape. By staying informed and steadfast in her commitment to her long-term financial strategy, Imaan was well-equipped to weather the ebb and flow of the financial markets on her path to achieving her goals.

Net Worth

Net worth is a crucial financial metric that provides a comprehensive snapshot of your individual financial position. It represents the difference between assets and liabilities, which is a measure of overall wealth and financial health. Net worth goes beyond just income or cash flow, as it considers both the value of all owned assets and accounts and outstanding debts and obligations.

Calculating net worth involves summing up all assets and subtracting all liabilities. Assets encompass a wide range of possessions, including cash, investments, real estate properties, vehicles, valuable possessions, and even intellectual property. Liabilities, on the other hand, consist of debts, loans, mortgages, credit card balances, and other financial obligations. By calculating net worth regularly, individuals and businesses can track their financial progress, assess their financial stability, and make informed decisions regarding investments, savings, and debt management.

Understanding net worth helps individuals evaluate their financial goals and plan for the future. Knowing your net worth allows you to identify opportunities to further eliminate debt that can improve your financial position. A positive net worth indicates accumulated wealth and a stronger financial position, which may provide opportunities for investment, retirement planning, and securing loans at favorable terms. On the other hand, a negative net worth implies excessive debts and financial liabilities, highlighting the need for debt reduction strategies and a more cautious approach to financial decision-making. Monitoring net worth over time allows for financial adjustments, wealth accumulation, and a clearer understanding of one's overall financial well-being.

Compound Returns

Albert Einstein once said, "Compound interest is the eighth wonder of the world. He who understands it, earns it; he who doesn't, pays it." Compounding is the ability of an asset to generate earnings, which are then reinvested or remain invested with the goal of generating their own earnings. The S&P 500 is a market-capitalization-weighted index of the 500 leading publicly traded companies in the U.S. The index has returned a historic annualized average return of around 11.88% since its 1957 inception through the end of 2021. Imaan regularly assumed an 11.88% rate of return for future goals and to illustrate the power of compounding. She realized that starting early is important to earnings. Here are a few examples she shared with friends:

- If you start at eighteen, invest $200/month and stop at 30. By the retirement age of 67, you will have over $3.7 million.
- If you start at thirty-five, invest $200/month, and don't stop until 67, at retirement you will have just $720,000.

Dividends

Dividends are a portion of a company's profit paid to shareholders. Public companies that pay dividends usually do so on a fixed schedule although they can issue them at any time. Dividends can be automatically reinvested into an asset to further accelerate growth in our returns.

Retirement Savings Accounts

Retirement savings accounts are specialized financial accounts that are designed to help individuals save and invest for their retirement years. These accounts offer various tax advantages and are subject to specific rules and regulations.

One popular type of retirement savings account is the Individual Retirement Account (IRA). There are two main types of IRAs: traditional IRAs and Roth IRAs. Contributions to a traditional IRA may be tax-deductible, and the investments in the account grow tax-deferred until withdrawal, at which point they are subject to income tax. Roth IRAs, on the other hand, are funded with after-tax dollars, and qualified withdrawals in retirement are tax-free. A simplified employee pension (SEP) IRA is another IRA that may be of interest to entrepreneurs. SEP IRAs are for self-employed or small business owners, and contributions are tax-deductible. With a SEP IRA you can contribute up to 25% of compensation for an employee or $66,000 per year (whatever is lesser). Proportional contributions for each eligible employee are required if the business owner contributes for themselves.

In addition to IRAs, many employers offer retirement savings accounts such as 401(k) plans or 403(b) plans. These plans allow employees to contribute a portion of their salary to the account on a pre-tax basis, meaning that the contributions are not taxed until withdrawal. Some employers even match a percentage of their employees' contributions, which can be a valuable benefit. Retirement savings accounts generally have contribution limits and withdrawal rules to ensure that the funds are primarily used for retirement purposes. It's important to consult with a financial advisor or tax professional to understand the specific rules and benefits associated with retirement savings accounts.

You are free to withdraw the contributions you made at any time under age 59 ½. Remember, you cannot withdraw the earnings, or else you will pay a penalty. However, if you're under 59 ½ and your ROTH IRA has been open for five years or more, your earnings will not be subjected to taxes if you meet one of the following conditions:

- You use the withdrawal (up to $10,000 lifetime maximum) to pay for a first-time home purchase.

- You use the withdrawal to pay for qualified education expenses.
- You use the withdrawal for qualified expenses related to a birth or adoption.
- You become disabled or pass away.
- You use the withdrawal to pay for unreimbursed medical expenses or health insurance if you're unemployed.

Imaan calculated that if she opened a ROTH IRA account with a starting balance of $2,000, contributing the maximum $6,500 per year, with an estimated 11.88% rate of return, in forty-five years over $9 million could be saved. In twenty-five years only $929,000 will be saved. She decided to start early.

Child Investment Readiness

One of Imaan's mentors even prepped her on how to have a newborn millionaire. Consider investing $1,000 at birth, assuming an 11.88 annual rate of return, the child at the retirement age of 67 will have $1.8 million. Investing $2,000 at birth, the child, at the standard retirement age of 67, will have over $3.6 million.

A ROTH IRA for minors account is another investment option for children if they have "income". Minors must have employment compensation. Qualifying income can come from a job or self-employment. IRA contributions cannot exceed a minor's earnings (if a minor earns $1,000 then only $1,000 can be contributed to the account. There is an annual maximum contribution of $6,000 per child, per year. Withdrawals can be used for education expenses with no penalty.

She also knows that investing can help your children get ahead on future education costs. When they are born, open a "529" plan with a broker. Contributing $250 per month into the 529 Plan and invest those funds into a broad ETF that can earn 10% per year (all tax-free). When they turn 18, they will have over $136,797 in their funds for their education costs.

9

Investment Portfolio Readiness

Imaan reviewed numerous investment vehicles and strategies and realized, that not everyone can do everything. With the help of her financial advisor, she developed an investment portfolio readiness checklist to help identify investment priorities and capabilities when considering income and financial freedom values. She shared it with friends and family once she had gotten a firm understanding of her investment strategies. But she always cautioned, that if you're uncertain or overwhelmed, consult with a financial advisor who can provide personalized guidance based on your unique circumstances and goals.

Research - Take the time to learn about different investment options, strategies, and financial markets. Understand the risks and rewards associated with each investment before committing your money.

Set Clear Goals - Define your investment goals and timeframe. Are you investing for retirement, buying a house, or funding your children's education? Knowing your objectives will help you make appropriate investment decisions.

Start with a Plan - Develop an investment plan that aligns with your goals and risk tolerance. Consider diversifying your portfolio by investing in different asset classes, such as high-yield savings, stocks, and real estate.

Start Small and Gradually Increase- Begin by investing a smaller amount of money to get comfortable with the process. As you gain confidence and experience, you can gradually increase your investment amount.

Automate - Pay yourself first! Schedule regular transfers from your bank account to your investment account. This ensures a consistent flow of funds for investment purposes. Most investment platforms allow you to set up automatic purchases of specific securities or funds. You can specify the amount and frequency of the investments, such as monthly or quarterly purchases.

Patience is Key - Investing is a long-term game. Avoid making impulsive decisions based on short-term market fluctuations. Stick to your plan and be patient, allowing your investments to grow over time.

Diversify Your Portfolio - Spreading your investments across different assets can help mitigate risks. By diversifying, you reduce the impact of a single investment's performance on your overall portfolio. Imaan learned about many metrics that are used to find good companies for a portfolio - *Revenue and Earnings*: Look at the company's revenue growth and profitability. Increasing revenue and consistent earnings indicate a healthy business. *Profit Margins*: Assess the company's gross profit margin, operating profit margin, and net profit margin. Higher margins indicate efficiency and profitability. *Return on Equity (ROE) and Return on Assets (ROA)*: These metrics measure the company's ability to generate returns for shareholders and efficiently use its assets to generate profits. *Debt Levels*: Evaluate the company's debt-to-equity ratio and total debt levels. Excessive debt can be a burden and may affect the company's financial stability. *Cash Flow*: Analyze the company's operating cash flow and free cash flow. Positive and growing cash flows indicate a strong financial position and the ability to invest in future growth. *Valuation Ratios*: Consider valuation metrics such as the price-to-earnings (P/E) ratio, price-to-sales (P/S) ratio, and price-to-book (P/B) ratio. Compare these ratios to industry peers and historical averages to assess whether the stock is overvalued or undervalued. *Dividend Yield*: If you are interested in income-generating stocks, check the company's dividend yield and its history of dividend payments. A consistent and growing dividend can be an attractive feature. *Market Capitalization*: Assess the company's market capitalization, which reflects its size and relative position in the market. Larger companies may offer more stability, while smaller companies may have higher growth potential. It's important to conduct thorough research or seek advice from a financial professional before making any investment decisions.

Regularly Review and Rebalance - Monitor your investments periodically and adjust if necessary. Rebalance your portfolio to maintain the desired asset allocation based on your risk tolerance and goals.

Don't Try to Time the Market - Timing the market consistently is extremely challenging, even for experienced investors. Instead, focus on the long-term trends and stay invested for the duration that aligns with your goals.

Consider Tax Implications - Understand the tax implications of your investments. Profits made on the sale of stock are taxable at either 0%, 15%, or 20% if you held the shares for more than 366 days. Anything held less than 366 days is considered short-term gains and is taxed at your ordinary tax rate. Also, some investment vehicles, like retirement accounts, offer tax advantages that can help you maximize your returns.

Once, Imaan received a $5,000 salary bonus and decided to invest it. She spread out her investments to create a balanced portfolio in the following manner. (This is not investment advice. Consult a financial advisor who can provide guidance based on your unique circumstances and goals):

- 30% into strong dividend stocks – stable companies with consistent growth
- 20% into mega-cap stocks - publicly-listed companies with a market capitalization value of more than $200 billion.
- 20% into high sales growth potential stocks
- 20% into a market index fund / ETF – Exposure to the overall market with consistent returns
- 5% into consumer defensive stocks – these companies have products that people will always have a need for
- 5% into safe havens – diversification while protecting against volatility and inflation.
  How long should you hold an investment? Warren Buffet said, "…when we own portions of outstanding businesses with outstanding managements, our favorite holding period is forever" Imaan defined the period long-term as an investment to be held for at least ten years. Investors have a long-term outlook and will hold shares of a company through market ups and downs. They don't care about today's stock price and avoid getting distracted by the hottest stocks. However, they are still able to make good decisions based on fundamental analysis. So, if a company used to be great, but no longer is, you should sell it and buy something that's becoming great.

10

Wealth Building

At the age of 30, Imaan confronted her most formidable challenge to date – a sudden and unexpected layoff from her job. The shock of this setback had the potential to erode her confidence, but Imaan was made of sterner stuff. Between her severance pay and fully funded financial shield, she refused to let this adversity defeat her.

Imaan demonstrated a remarkable ability to adapt and persevere because of her discipline and financial risk management. Instead of fretting about money every day, she was able to focus on important next steps. She leveraged her skills and tapped into her network, exploring new horizons for employment and even contemplating the prospect of starting her own business. Once again, her resilience became her defining quality during this period.

She harnessed her passion and expertise for international political analysis and coupled it with her entrepreneurial spirit to launch her very own consultancy firm. Through dedication and a commitment to excellence, her business became very successful. As her business profits grew, she remembered that increasing cash flow is crucial to wealth building. The goal is to ensure that more of your income is coming from passive sources. This income should be used to invest in assets that pay you. Imaan looked for other growth opportunities which allowed her to invest more in passive income streams. Her journey reminds us that, even in the face of adversity, there is always a path forward, and it is through discipline and determination that we forge our own destiny.

Imaan was goal-setting one day and determined that if she could earn $400 profit a day from an additional income stream and invest it, that would be $1.8 million in 10 years. Small wins add up. The ideal goal is to generate enough passive income that allows you to fulfill your needs, and possibly reach the point where you can retire early and "fire her boss".

Embracing the concept of passive income, Imaan displayed a forward-thinking approach by seeking out opportunities beyond her primary business venture. She ventured into diverse avenues, driven by the belief that there was more to financial security than just a primary successful income stream, even though she was now the founder of a startup.

She began a blog, sharing her insights and knowledge with a wider audience. This not only allowed her to express her passion for political analysis but also created an additional income stream through paid subscriptions. Her entrepreneurial spirit led her to write an e-book on political strategy, further enhancing her financial portfolio.

But Imaan didn't stop there. She understood the potential of real estate as a source of passive income. With a strategic investment mindset, she entered the world of real estate, expanding her financial horizons even further. These endeavors gradually started to generate additional income streams, steadily fueling her journey toward financial independence.

Imaan's story is a testament to the idea that financial security can be achieved by diversifying one's income sources and adopting an entrepreneurial mindset. It's a reminder that there are opportunities all around us, waiting to be harnessed with determination and foresight, offering the promise of a more secure and prosperous future.

- $100/day equals $25,000 per year
- $200/day equals $50,000 per year

- $300/day equals $75,000 per year
- $400/day equals a six-figure salary

Whispers of the Wealthy

Imaan would often ponder the secrets of wealthy families that set them apart from others. She was not all that concerned about the material items that rich people had, but more so the process they undertook to preserve their wealth. The keys to their success aren't typically displayed on billboards for all to see, yet through her research and growing network of influential individuals, she understood that this knowledge isn't an exclusive domain reserved for only a select few families worldwide. Yes, it's shared quietly within families but also passed down from mentors to proteges. This wisdom isn't solely about money and investments; it goes much deeper. It's about the mindset, the habits, and the strategies that distinguish the wealthy.

It's about thinking big, daring to take calculated risks, and maintaining a perpetual quest for opportunities. It's an appreciation for the virtues of patience, discipline, and unwavering perseverance that act as a foundation of their achievements.

After interviewing the truly wealthy members of her network on the subject, she jotted down six wealth-wise tactics that can guide her on the path toward financial freedom. Over time, she fleshed them out into actionable goals. She realized that not all of the strategies would be applicable to her current stage in life, but as she continued to develop, they may be attainable. She told herself not to be disheartened if there was something on the list that she could not implement today. By taking these wealth-wise steps, she could build a foundation that may allow her to execute them in the future.

One purpose of developing this wealth roadmap was when she realized that wealth isn't just about amassing riches. It's also about the legacy we leave behind, passing on not only our wealth but also knowledge to future generations. By sharing her wisdom, she could equip them with the tools and insights they need to navigate the complex world of finance and make sound financial decisions. In this way, she was investing in the prosperity of her descendants, ensuring that they, too, could execute these wealth-wise tactics because of the wisdom she'd impart.

Wealth-wise Tactic #1: Save 50% percent of your income for seven years.

Saving 50% of your income for seven years can have numerous benefits. Here are three significant advantages:

1. Financial Independence and Security: By saving half of your income consistently, you build a substantial financial cushion. This approach allows you to achieve financial independence faster than most people who live paycheck to paycheck or have little savings. By accumulating a significant amount of money over seven years, you create a financial shield that can protect you from unexpected expenses, job loss, or economic downturns. This financial security gives you peace of mind and the freedom to make choices based on your values and long-term goals.

2. Accelerated Wealth Building: Saving half of your income for an extended period can lead to accelerated wealth accumulation. The power of compound returns comes into play as your assets grow over time. By consistently saving a substantial portion of your income, you can invest those savings wisely in assets such as stocks, bonds, real estate, or businesses. Compounding returns over seven years can significantly boost your net worth, helping you achieve your financial goals more quickly, whether it's early retirement, starting a business, or pursuing other dreams.

3. Flexibility and Opportunities: Saving 50% of your income creates a significant surplus that provides you with more flexibility and opportunities in the future. With a healthy savings

cushion, you have the freedom to take calculated risks, explore new career paths, or embark on entrepreneurial ventures. It can also give you the ability to travel, pursue further education, or support causes you care about. Saving diligently for seven years allows you to create a solid foundation for your financial future, enabling you to seize opportunities that may arise and make choices based on what truly matters to you. Achieving a 50% savings rate requires discipline, planning, and prioritization of your expenses. It's important to create a budget, track your spending, and make intentional decisions about how you allocate your income.

Wealth-wise Tactic #2: In a two-income household, live off 25% and invest 75%.

Living off 25% of their income while investing 75% can be an ambitious financial goal for a married couple in a two-income household. But here are three ways they could achieve this:

- ○ Budgeting and Expense Reduction: Creating a comprehensive budget is crucial for managing finances effectively. The couple should track their income and expenses to identify areas where they can cut back. They can start by analyzing their spending patterns and identifying non-essential or duplicate expenses they can eliminate or reduce. This is less about dining out less frequently and reducing entertainment expenses, and more about fast-tracking the elimination of the housing expense and student loans. By being mindful of their spending and prioritizing needs over wants, they can also maximize the amount available for investment.
- ○ Increase Income and Save the Difference: Finding ways to increase their income can have a significant impact on

their ability to invest a higher percentage. They can explore options such as negotiating a raise at work, taking up a side gig or freelance work, or investing in personal and professional development to enhance their earning potential. If they can generate additional income, they should save and invest the difference rather than increase their expenses. This approach allows them to maintain their current lifestyle while channeling more funds toward buying assets that will produce more income.

○ Optimize Tax Strategies: Understanding and utilizing tax strategies can help the couple optimize their investment potential. They can consult with a financial advisor or tax professional to explore options like contributing to tax-advantaged retirement accounts. By taking advantage of tax deductions and credits available to them, they can reduce their taxable income and potentially increase the portion available for investment. Additionally, they can review their tax withholding to ensure they are not overpaying and adjust them accordingly.

It's important for the couple to have clear investment goals and develop a well-diversified investment portfolio. They should consider working with a financial advisor to assess their risk tolerance, and investment options, and develop a long-term investment strategy that aligns with their goals. Individual circumstances may vary, and it's always advisable to seek professional financial advice tailored to your specific situation.

Wealth-wise Tactic #3: When you sell a business, negotiate a 5% royalty of gross revenue over a decade.

Building a business and then selling it is akin to giving money away. However, sealing a deal with future royalties is advantageous for you as a seller. Here are some reasons why this arrangement is important:

1. Continuity of Income: By negotiating a royalty based on a percentage of gross revenue, the seller ensures a continuous stream of income even after selling the business. This can be particularly beneficial if the seller still holds intellectual property rights or has ongoing involvement in the business. It allows them to maintain a vested interest and receive a share of the profits generated by the business they built.

2. Risk Mitigation: The royalty arrangement can serve as a risk mitigation strategy for the buyer. Instead of paying a large lump sum upfront, the buyer can spread the payments over a defined period based on the business's performance. If the business does well, the royalty payments reflect its success, but if it underperforms, the buyer's financial liability is reduced. This structure aligns the buyer's financial commitment with the business's performance.

3. Supporting the Business post-sale: The royalty arrangement can motivate the seller to support the success of the business even after the sale. Since the seller has a stake in the business's performance through the royalty payments, they may be motivated to provide ongoing assistance, guidance, or expertise to ensure the business continues to thrive. This can be particularly valuable if the seller possesses unique knowledge or has built strong customer relationships that contribute to the business's success.

4. Flexibility and Negotiation: Negotiating the royalty percentage and duration allows both parties to find a mutually beneficial arrangement. The specific terms can be tailored to suit the unique characteristics of the business, the buyer's financial capacity, and the seller's goals. This flexibility in negotiation enables a fair and customized agreement that satisfies both parties' needs and interests.

The appropriateness of a royalty arrangement can depend on various factors, including the nature of the business, industry norms, market conditions, and the specific circumstances of the buyer and seller. Consulting with legal and financial professionals experienced in business transactions is essential to ensure that all aspects of the agreement are thoroughly assessed and properly structured to protect the interests of both parties.

Wealth-wise Tactic #4: Develop seven revenue streams.

The average millionaire has seven streams of income. Here are 10 examples of common revenue streams:

1. Salary or Wages: The most common and reliable revenue stream for many individuals is income from employment or self-employment. This is typically earned through regular employment and a consistent paycheck.

2. Business Income: Operating a business or being a business owner can generate income through sales of products or services. This can involve traditional brick-and-mortar businesses, online ventures, or freelancing.

3. Freelancing or Consulting: Offering services as a freelancer or consultant in a specific field or area of expertise can provide additional income. This could include writing, graphic design, web development, marketing, tutoring, or coaching.

4. Rental Income: If you own property, you can generate revenue by renting out a spare room, an apartment, your backyard pool, or even your entire property on platforms like Airbnb or through traditional long-term leases.

5. Investment Income: This includes passive earnings from investments, such as dividends from stocks, mutual funds, index funds, growth from savings instruments, and capital

gains from selling investments at a profit. Dividends are typically paid out by profitable companies to their shareholders. This involves growing your wealth over time by letting your investments work for you.

6. Royalties on IP: If you have creative or intellectual property, such as books, music, or patents, you can earn royalties by licensing or selling the rights to use your work.

7. Online Courses or E-Learning: Creating and selling online courses or educational content can be a lucrative revenue stream. Platforms like Udemy and Teachable allow you to reach a wide audience and monetize your knowledge.

8. Affiliate Marketing: By promoting products or services through affiliate links on your website, blog, or social media channels, you can earn commissions for each sale or referral generated.

9. E-commerce: Starting an online store or selling products through platforms like Etsy or Amazon can be a viable revenue stream. This can involve selling physical products, digital goods, or even drop shipping.

10. Real Estate Investment: Investing in real estate properties for rental income or capital appreciation can provide long-term revenue streams. Owning and renting out real estate properties can provide a stream of income through monthly rental payments. This can include residential properties, commercial properties, or vacation rentals. This could also include real estate investment trusts (REITs) or real estate crowdfunding platforms.

Remember that generating revenue streams requires effort, dedication, and sometimes initial investment. It's essential to assess your skills, interests, and resources to determine which revenue streams are most suitable for you. Additionally, consulting with financial professionals can provide valuable guidance and advice tailored to your specific financial goals and circumstances.

Wealth-wise Tactic #5: Find a way to invest/buy into ten private companies.

If you don't have a lot of capital, offer up an arrangement to perform a service for equity. Help them reach their goals. It's a win-win situation where you offer your skills, expertise, or services to a company in exchange for a stake in the business. This approach allows you to contribute your time and effort instead of a large financial investment. Identify the specific skills or services you can offer. It could be anything from graphic design and writing to programming or social media management. Determine your niche and focus on areas where you excel. Define the services you're offering and specify the scope, delivery time, and any extras you can provide. Pricing is important, so research the market rates for similar services to ensure your prices are competitive. Continuously refine your skills, keep up with industry trends, and actively seek feedback to enhance your services. With persistence and a strong work ethic, you can turn your expertise into profitable ventures. Make sure to get any arrangement with the company in writing. First, identify a company that aligns with your interests and where you believe you can add value. Reach out to the founders or decision-makers and put your deal on the table. Highlight how your specific skills or services can benefit the company's growth and success. Once you establish an agreement, the terms can vary depending on the company and your negotiation skills. You could receive equity in the form of stocks, options, or a percentage of ownership. Keep in mind that the amount of equity you receive will depend on the value you bring and the company's overall valuation. It's essential to approach such arrangements with caution and conduct thorough research on the company, its potential for growth, and its management team. Additionally, consult with a legal professional to ensure that the agreement is properly structured, protecting both your interests and the company's. Remember, this path requires not only a belief in the company's potential but also a commitment to delivering on your promises.

By leveraging your skills and services for equity, you can become an integral part of a company's success story while gaining a stake in its future growth.

Wealth-wise Tactic #6: Acquire 10,000 shares of a company in your portfolio.

The importance of buying 10,000 shares depends on the individual's net worth, financial goals, and risk tolerance. Here are a couple of reasons why a high-net-worth individual might consider buying a significant number of shares:

1. Potential for higher returns: Owning a larger number of shares means that any price appreciation or dividend payments would substantially impact the overall investment return. If the stock performs well, a larger shareholding could potentially lead to higher profits. At a quarterly dividend payment of $.24/share of Apple stock, 10,000 shares would yield $9,600 yearly just on dividend payments alone. When speaking to others, Imaan would often use this example to illustrate the impact dividend payments can have on your wealth equation: In 2023, Time Cook, CEO of Apple will make $49 million. Warren Buffet will receive almost $860 million in dividend payments from his Apple holdings!

2. Trading liquidity: Stocks with high trading volumes tend to have greater liquidity, meaning it is easier to buy or sell large quantities of shares without significantly impacting the stock's price. For investors who frequently trade or engage in short-term strategies, having a larger number of shares can facilitate smoother transactions.

   However, it's important to approach investing with careful consideration and not solely focus on the number of shares owned. Factors such as the company's fundamentals, financial health, industry outlook, and overall market conditions should be thoroughly assessed. Additionally, diversifying across multiple stocks and asset classes can help reduce exposure to specific risks associated with a single stock. It is always recommended to consult with a financial advisor or do thorough research before making investment decisions.

Eliminate Your Housing Expense

Another underlying current in Imaan's understanding of accelerated wealth building was eliminating her housing expense. Her opinion was that contrary to popular belief "owning" a primary residency is not a useful asset until you pay off the mortgage completely. Obviously, it serves a purpose by sheltering you and your family. But until the mortgage is paid, it can be an illiquid asset when mortgage rates are high. Interest-bearing mortgages are a huge liability, in addition to insurance, repairs, and property taxes. The word mortgage has the following linguistic roots.

- ○ *Origin Latin mortuus = dead ->*
- ○ *Old French mort (dead) + gage (pledge)*
- ○ *Mortgage = death pledge*

It's in the interest of lenders to keep homeowners in a perpetual condition of having a mortgage. However, eliminating Imaan's housing expense was the key to building wealth for herself and future generations. A common rule of thumb is that up to one-third of after-tax income will be spent on housing needs. Generating enough passive income to cover rent or mortgage expenses frees up a huge amount of hard-earned income to fund your values and buy other income-producing assets. One passive income strategy she started developing was buying enough dividend-paying stocks to cover the expense on a quarterly or monthly basis. She decided that she would continue to explore ways to eliminate her housing expense in addition to other topics such as trusts and inheritance.

11

It's A Journey

As years passed, Imaan's disciplined approach to investing paid off. She accumulated substantial wealth, allowing her financial goals to be achieved and enjoy a comfortable lifestyle. By age 40, Imaan achieved her vision of financial freedom. Her investments flourished, passive income flowed steadily, and she sold her consultancy firm at a premium because of the respected brand she built in the industry. She looked back on her journey with pride, grateful for the lessons learned, and the mentors who guided her. Imaan built upon the mindset passed down from her mother. Her dedication served as an inspiration to her friends and family, demonstrating the power of knowledge, discipline, and long-term strategy in the world of finance.

She decided to coin the term, "wealth-wise" as a means to describing the mind state she started developing those many years ago on Boston College's campus. First, wealth-wise is about arming yourself with a distinct set of tools: specific knowledge, accountability, and leverage. It's not merely about counting the years in your life; it's about infusing life into every one of those years.

This specific knowledge can't be readily acquired through traditional training. It's not just about understanding the ins and outs of financial markets; it's also about knowing yourself deeply. If society can train you, it can train someone else and, just like that, replace you.

Specific knowledge is discovered when you follow your true passions and interests rather than blindly chasing the latest trends.

Next, being wealth-wise is being accountable and prepared to take calculated risks that you can manage independently. Successful risk-taking leads to rewards such as responsibility, equity, and leverage. Also, leverage is the key to immense wealth, but remember the distinction between bad debt and leverage. Business leverage can come from capital, labor, and products that have no cost of replication, like code and media.

Labor, on the other hand, involves people working for you. While labor leverage might impress some, Imaan didn't make it a priority to attain a large workforce. It is an expensive resource. Imaan came to the conclusion that the real secret to breaking away from the pack and becoming an innovator is in code and media development, which are self-service leverage tools used by many newly successful ventures and innovators. Anyone can create software and media assets that work for you while you sleep.

Coding wasn't Imaan's forte, but she understood its power and leveraged it by outsourcing projects that advanced her ideas. You can write books, and blogs, or create videos and podcasts. Leverage is a force multiplier. Would you rather invest $1,000 of your own money or $10,000 of someone else's? You can work on a project for a year by yourself or collaborate with a team of ten for the same duration. You can offer advice to a single friend or reach out to the masses through social media.

Imaan's journey didn't end with her own financial freedom; it had only just begun. She decided to share her knowledge and experiences with others, mentoring young graduates on their paths to financial independence. But her enthusiasm for teaching soon led her onto the next leg of her journey. She decided to open a school in Senegal, educating youth on finance, community wealth building, and of course, leadership in politics. She would continue to inspire countless others to embark on their own trek to pursue their purpose.